THE ESSENTIAL SHAKESPEARE

05369

THE GRAFTON PORTRAIT

THE ESSENTIAL
SHAKESPEARE

A BIOGRAPHICAL ADVENTURE

BY

J. DOVER WILSON

*Our stability is but balance, and wisdom lies
In masterful administration of the unforeseen.*
BRIDGES

*Shakespeare led a life of Allegory: his works
are the comments on it.* KEATS

CAMBRIDGE
AT THE UNIVERSITY PRESS
1960

PUBLISHED BY
THE SYNDICS OF THE CAMBRIDGE UNIVERSITY PRESS

Bentley House, 200 Euston Road, London, N.W. 1
American Branch: 32 East 57th Street, New York 22, N.Y.

First edition	*April*	1932
Reprinted	*July*	1932
,,	*Jan.*	1933
,,	*Feb.*	1935
,,	*Sept.*	1937
,,		1942, 1943,
		1945, 1946,
		1948, 1952,
First paperback edition		1960

PRINTED IN THE U.S.A.

CONTENTS

The Grafton Portrait   *frontispiece*

I   Images of Shakespeare   *page* 1

II   The Elizabethan Scene   15

III   Enter William Shakespeare with divers of worship   38

IV   Comedy and Character   68

V   History and Politics   92

VI   The Razor-Edge   108

VII   The Enchanted Island   128

References and Notes   146

Note. The frontispiece is reproduced, by permission of the John Rylands Librarian, from a portrait of an unknown man, Shakespeare's exact contemporary. It was first discovered in 1907, at Winston-on-Tees, near Darlington and now hangs in the Rylands Library, Manchester; it is known as the 'Grafton Portrait' because it originally came from Grafton Regis, Northamptonshire.

PREFACE

I HAVE to thank the Council of the British Academy for its kind permission to reprint one or two brief passages from a lecture I delivered before that body in 1929, entitled *The Elizabethan Shakespeare*.

In a book of this scope and size it would be absurd to attempt a record of my indebtedness to previous writers: let it suffice to say that my creditors are more than I can number and the liability beyond my discharge. But two names I must mention. I had hoped to break a lance with an old friend of Cambridge days, Lytton Strachey, in the last chapter, which was first written as a reply to his brilliant essay, *Shakespeare's Final Period*. But just as I was going to press, he laid his pen aside to join "the loveliest and the best", and I have removed all traces of disagreement except one nameless reference.

I could wish to associate the last chapter too with the name of Sir Edmund Chambers. Though of course the book as a whole owes more than I can estimate to his *William Shakespeare: a study of facts and problems*, I admit to my shame that it was not until it was all but complete, and my theory of *The Tempest* and of what he calls Shakespeare's "conversion" had been worked out, that I read his early prefaces, recently reprinted as *Shakespeare: a survey*. It was interesting to discover that in respect to the last phase we were on somewhat the same tack, and though I differ with him sharply on certain important details, as he no doubt will with me, I derive much encouragement from our measure of agreement.

I hope my title will not be misunderstood. "Here, in a nutshell, is the kind of man I believe Shakespeare to have been", is what it is intended to convey. I might perhaps have called it "A credible Shakespeare".

J. D. W.

February, 1932

WHAT IS A POET?

He is a man speaking to men: a man, it is true, endued with more lively sensibility, more enthusiasm and tenderness, who has a greater knowledge of human nature, and a more comprehensive soul, than are supposed to be common among mankind; a man pleased with his own passions and volitions, and who rejoices more than other men in the spirit of life that is in him; delighting to contemplate similar volitions and passions as manifested in the goings-on of the Universe, and habitually impelled to create them where he does not find them.

WORDSWORTH

I

IMAGES OF SHAKESPEARE

Look here upon this picture and on this
Hamlet.

THIS LITTLE BOOK attempts, as many hundreds
before it have attempted, to interpret the career of
William Shakespeare, poet and dramatist for all
time, and principal entertainer of Elizabethan and
Jacobean London. And if I am asked what excuse
I offer for adding even one more pebble to the
enormous cairn of commentary and biography
beneath which the real Shakespeare somewhere
lies, I can only reply that I heartily dislike some of
the current interpretations which pass as orthodox,
and have long wished to work out another which
might seem more in accord at once with common
sense and with what we know of the life and spirit
of other poets and creative artists.

My own interpretation is of course influenced by
personal prepossessions, as all general notions of
Shakespeare must be, but I can at least claim that it
is no piece of preconceived sentimentalism. Rather,
it has revealed itself bit by bit through a study of
the plays, of the period and of the known facts of the
life, a study carried on continuously for over thirty
years and culminating during the last ten of them in
the most intimate relationship which anyone, not
an actor and dramatist of genius like Mr Granville
Barker, can now have with Shakespeare; I mean
the editing of his works from the originals. It is true

that the edition I am concerned with has so far embraced the Comedies only,[1] but this in some degree puts me at an advantage, since it means at any rate that I start at the right end, the Elizabethan end; most previous biographers, to my thinking, having gone astray by considering Shakespeare too much from the standpoint of his later work, written during the reign of James I.

The sublimity of his subject, and the comparative poverty of contemporary information about it, expose anyone who undertakes to write a life of Shakespeare to many perils, but the greatest of them all is the personal equation. It is indeed impossible that he should altogether escape it; for he must begin by framing some general conception of what he takes to be Shakespeare's spirit and personality, which is as if a blind man who could not climb should try to form a general idea of the Matterhorn or Mont Blanc from every point of view and in all weather conditions. Yet he may observe two precautions which will go some way towards saving him from absolute disaster. In the first place he should make all possible and legitimate use of the lives of other poets and artists to throw light upon the life of Shakespeare, acquainting himself as well with what other poets and artists have thought about their greatest fellow, since such thoughts will be of infinitely more value than anything he could excogitate out of his own feeble imagination. And secondly he should do what in him lies to make clear both to himself and to his readers what personal prepossessions about Shake-

[1] Written in 1931.

speare he starts with. Every biographer has them, though few confess them, and most are unconscious of them. I observe that even Sir Edmund Chambers, who appears in his *William Shakespeare: a study of facts and problems* as an arch-sceptic and a sardonic anti-romantic, when composing his earlier book, *Shakespeare: a survey*, followed Sidney's precept "Look in thy heart and write" and found an image there, which is certainly not lacking in romance.

I shall disclose my own image of Shakespeare towards the end of this chapter. At the moment I would insist that this secret image of the heart, of which the biographer may be completely unaware, is too often the root cause of his aberration. What may be called the scientific school of Shakespearian biography furnishes an excellent example. Setting the plays and poems aside as "impersonal" and therefore of no value whatever as evidence, they proceed to build up every available scrap of external information into their structure, without realising that the significance they attach to each scrap depends upon their own implicit conception of the poet, and that the scraps can only be held together by a plentiful supply of mortar in the form of suppressed hypothesis. The best known writer of the school is Sidney Lee, whose magisterial *Life of William Shakespeare* is the standard authority upon the subject. An indispensable reference book of facts, which I shall not hesitate to make use of in the following pages, it offers reading encouraging to the industrious apprentice and flattering to the

3

successful business man; for its theme is the story of the butcher-boy of Stratford who made a fortune in London, and the conclusion it draws is that "his literary attainments and successes were chiefly valued as serving the prosaic end of making a permanent provision for himself and his daughters"; which is like saying that Keats wrote the *Ode to a Nightingale* in order to have something in his stocking against a rainy day with Fanny Brawne. Such writers are dangerous because their show of objectivity and science may conceal their premises from the very elect. The image in Lee's heart was that of a typical English manufacturer who happened to deal in *Twelfth Nights* and *Lears* instead of brass tacks. Now Lee himself was not in the least like this. Where then did his image come from? An unimaginative man, he was not likely to have invented it. As we shall see in Chapter III, he got it partly from an earlier biographer, Halliwell-Phillipps; but he also paid frequent visits to Stratford, and there he had ample opportunities of gazing at a false image which would suggest all the ideas he required. In a word, the *Life* that Lee gave us was not the life of William Shakespeare the man and the poet, but the life that 'William Shakespeare', the bust in Stratford Church, might have lived had he ever existed in flesh and blood.

The Stratford bust is the only portrait of the poet which can claim any sort of authority, seeing that the Droeshout frontispiece to the First Folio is nothing but a clumsy engraving derived from it, and that all other portraits are themselves derived from either the bust or the engraving. Moreover the monument was erected at Stratford shortly after Shakespeare's death, before 1623 at any rate, and it is generally supposed that the features were modelled directly from a mask taken from Shakespeare's face, alive or dead. Yet, despite everything, I make bold to say that this bust is one of the greatest of all obstacles to the true understanding of Shakespeare. Here are a few descriptive notes of it from a learned essay by Mr M. H. Spielmann, which is objective but by no means hostile in spirit: "its wooden appearance and vapid expression", "its coarsely-shaped, half-moon eyebrows, more like George Robey's than anybody else's", its staring eyes set "too close together" and like the nose "too small for the face". The essay also draws attention to the extraordinary upper lip, the hanging lower lip, and the general air of stupid and self-complacent prosperity. All this might suit well enough with an affluent and retired butcher, but does gross wrong to the dead poet. "Some men there are love not a gaping pig", and for half the unlearned world this Shakespeare simply will not do. The Stratford bust, and Lee's *Life* inspired by gazing too much upon it, are together, I am convinced, mainly responsible for the campaign against "the man of Stratford" and the attempts to dethrone him in favour of Lord Bacon, the Earl of Derby, the Earl of Oxford, the Earl of Rutland, or whatever coroneted pretender may be in vogue at the present moment.

Yet the bust is easily explained. It is the old story, only too familiar to friends and relatives of most men wealthy or famous enough to fall a prey to the second-rate portrait-painter. The job was given to an Anglo-Flemish mason of London, one Garratt Janssen, who knew what belonged to a monument and executed the task in a workman-like and (as monuments go) highly creditable fashion. The proportions are admirable, and the architectural design, with its pillars and canopy, its mantled shield, and its twin cherubs, is even beautiful. But one thing was clearly quite beyond the workman's scope —the human face, the face that happened to be Shakespeare's! And if Mistress Shakespeare and the poet's daughters disliked the portrait, what could they do? In cases of this kind, the family of the victim is helpless. There was the monument, complete and no doubt paid for, paid for perhaps by friends as well as relatives. And what a fine monument it was—all but the face! As to that, widow and daughters could only grin, like the travesty that confronted them, and bear it.

But we need not; and it is time an end was put to the scandal of three centuries. For Janssen's self-satisfied pork-butcher and the Folio engraving taken from it, which Sir John Squire has called "the pudding-faced effigy of Droeshout", stand between us and the true Shakespeare, and are so obviously false images of the greatest poet of all time that the world turns from them in disgust and thinks it is turning from Shakespeare himself. A banner of the crusade against Janssen and Droeshout is hoisted in the frontispiece to this book. It is a reproduction of a beautiful portrait, now hanging in the Rylands

6

Library at Manchester, of a young man of Shakespeare's time. As the inscription at the top shows, he was Shakespeare's exact contemporary, and a comparison with the Droeshout engraving reveals the further coincidence that the relative distances from the chin to the lower lip, from the lower lip to the tip of the nose, from the tip of the nose to the lower eyelid, from the lower eyelid to the eyebrow, and from the eyebrow to the top of the forehead, are identical in both portraits, a fact which is not to be despised seeing that honest Droeshout and Janssen would take a pride in getting their faces right "by the squier". The similarity too of the great foreheads is particularly striking. Beyond these coincidences there is nothing whatever to connect the unknown youth of the wonderful eyes and the oval Shelley-like face with the poet who was also twenty-four years old in 1588.

Of course, the picture has been claimed as a genuine Shakespeare portrait. The temptation so to claim it is almost irresistible; and for my part since I first had it brought to my notice in 1914, the temptation has grown stronger every time I have looked at it. It was encouraging also to learn from his posthumous book published in 1928 that Dr John Smart of Glasgow, the sanest of modern Shakespearian biographers, "found in it his own idea of the youthful Shakespeare and wished it genuine". Yet there is no real evidence, and I do not ask the reader to believe in it or even to wish to believe in it. All I suggest is that he may find it useful in trying to frame his own image of

7

Shakespeare. It will at any rate help him to forget the Stratford bust. Let him take it, if he will, as a painted cloth or arras, drawn in front of that monstrosity, and symbolising the Essential Poet. A portrait of Keats or Shelley would have served the purpose; but since fortune has preserved it for us, this picture of an unknown Elizabethan poet serves better. "I think", wrote Keats humbly, "I shall be among the English poets after my death", and Matthew Arnold cried out upon this "He is; he is with Shakespeare". We are apt to forget at times, in our preoccupation with Shakespeare the Stratford Institution, Shakespeare the National Bard, or even Shakespeare the world-worshipped dramatic interpreter of mankind, that Shakespeare himself is also "among the English poets", is with Keats and with Shelley. If my frontispiece reminds even one reader of this, it will not be altogether impertinent.

It may remind readers of another thing, which is still more often forgotten: Shakespeare was once young. Indeed, he was never old; for he gave up writing at forty-eight and was only fifty-two when he died. Yet for most people he is a kind of Grand Old Man of literature. This is due, partly to the Stratford bust, but chiefly I think to the general trend of Shakespearian criticism since Coleridge, which has concentrated upon the tragedies and later plays like *The Tempest*, and has left the comedies and histories in comparative neglect. Thus we have come to look at Shakespeare through the wrong end of the biographical telescope, to think of him as pre-eminently a tragic poet, facing the

vastidity of the universe, wrestling with the problems of evil and disaster—as a man, in short,
of brooding temper, of lofty thought, of grave de-
meanour, and, after passing through the cleansing
fires, of cheerful serenity of mind. This Olympian
vision might do perhaps for Goethe, who seemed
Athene-like to spring into the world in full panoply
of philosophic calm, but Shakespeare I am convinced never at any time of his life even remotely
resembled it.

The tragic Shakespeare, as we shall see, was
a suffering Shakespeare; and the serenity of *The
Tempest* was rather the serenity of recovery after
sickness, or of peace after a hurricane, than anything aloof or pontifical. Shakespeare was more
akin to Dostoieffsky than to Goethe; or perhaps
it is better to think of him as a kind of larger
and happier Keats who lived on to tread the *via
dolorosa* that Dostoieffsky alone of the moderns has
trodden after him. For the Keats and the Dostoieffsky within him, were only part-tenants of an all-
human spirit, which expressed itself during most of
the first half of his dramatic career in comedy without a parallel in the world's literature for gaiety of
heart. Thus when Dr A. C. Bradley, after insisting
that "Keats was of Shakespeare's tribe", goes on to
suggest that "in quality—and I speak of nothing
else—the mind of Shakespeare at three-and-twenty
may not have been very different", we gratefully
subscribe as regards the creator of Romeo, Juliet,
King Richard the Second, *Lucrece* and Oberon's
fairy-land, while insisting in our turn that the mind

which produced Mercutio, *Love's Labour's Lost*, and Bottom possessed qualities of steel-like brilliance and temper, of self-assurance and poise, of a blithe and delighted acceptance of Life in all its manifestations, which we look for in vain in Keats.

By leaving the comic muse out of the picture, the Victorian image of Shakespeare as the sedate Olympian does him much dishonour, for it means robbing him of a good third of his laurels and ignoring the miracle of his spiritual development. The Comedies came first; the Shakespeare of *King Lear* and *The Tempest* grew out of the Shakespeare who gave us Berowne and the Bastard, Juliet's Nurse and Mistress Quickly, the clowns Lance and Lancelot, Sir Toby Belch and Sir John Falstaff, to name only a few of the greatest rout of unseemly, and often indecent, disreputables that ever teemed from a dramatist's brain. And though the Jacobean Shakespeare became more serious than the Elizabethan, he was never, right up to the end, a whit more "respectable". As for the comedies themselves, with all the verve and gusto of their gay indecorum, who that reads them can doubt that they have been cast up on the shores of time by the most impetuous tide of warm-blooded humanity that ever beat through the heart of man? They are immortal, because of their amazing vitality; and their vitality is an indisputable testimony to the enormous satisfaction that went to their making. Shakespeare wrote to please. "The poet", and it is Wordsworth who speaks, "writes under one restriction only, namely the necessity of giving immediate pleasure."

Shakespeare, therefore, wrote to please his audience. But first and foremost and all the time, he wrote to please himself.

One more false image, and I have done with them—the image of the "impersonal" Shakespeare, of a Shakespeare who keeps himself out of his writings, not excepting the *Sonnets*. It is an aspect of the Olympian Shakespeare we have just been considering, and has been made much of by the "scientific" school of biography because it relieves them of the necessity of checking their notions by the evidence of the plays and the poems. After what has just been said, I shall content myself with a few observations on a single point only.

Elizabethan drama was a social institution which performed many functions since taken over by more specialised agencies. Among other things it was, like the modern newspaper, at once the focus and the purveyor of the London gossip of the day. In a word, it was topical. Now Sidney Lee and those who follow him, insist that here Shakespeare differed from his fellow dramatists, that he preserved himself in this as in other respects unspotted from his world. In taking this line they are to some extent reacting from the extravagancies of F. G. Fleay, who seems to have found little except topicality in Shakespeare's plays. Yet they err as far on one side as he did on the other. Hamlet tells us, and in this Shakespeare is surely for once at any rate speaking through the lips of a character, that "the purpose of playing", which of course includes the purpose of the dramatist, "is, as 'twere to hold the mirror up to nature, to show virtue her own feature, scorn her own image, and the very age and body of the time his form and pressure". That is the gist of the matter, both then and now. Shakespeare's plays reflect the passing intellectual and social fashions of his day as the plays of Bernard Shaw do of ours, and Shakespeare never minded in the least glancing at events or persons which were at the moment agitating the minds of his audience. No one can deny that he refers to the "war of the theatres" in the second act of *Hamlet*, or to the Irish campaign of Essex in one of the choruses of *Henry V*, or to the "dead shepherd" Marlowe in *As You Like It*, or to some entertainment given to Queen Elizabeth in the speech about the "little western flower" in *A Midsummer-Night's Dream*, or to the trial of the Jesuit, Henry Garnet, in the Porter's speech in *Macbeth*, or that the wreck of the "Sea Adventure" off an island in the Bermudas in 1609 gave him his idea for *The Tempest*—and so one could go on.

It is certain then that Shakespeare did not deliberately avoid topical allusion, as those who worship the Olympian claim. And if so, may we not suspect allusion and reference in many passages where it has hitherto not been detected? We not only may but should; for, once again, the essential Shakespeare will be altogether misconceived if we think of him as one who stood apart from the life of his time. On the contrary, we may look for him at the very heart of that life, and picture his eager spirit following the doings of Essex and Raleigh, of

Drake and Roger Williams, of Francis Bacon and Robert Cecil, with the keenest possible interest. Not "his tragic life-story", of which we know nothing, but the life at the courts of Elizabeth and James, the persons and doings of the great men of the land, the political and social events of the hour— these form the real background of his plays. But we must be careful not to be too crude or too literal in this matter, or we may fall into the trap that confounded Fleay. Shakespeare was a dramatic artist not a journalist, and above all he was subtle. He hardly ever goes out of his way to make a topical hit; he glances at the business in passing, obliquely and in hints, rather than by overt reference. And in so doing he showed a double wisdom: first, he escaped the troubles which fell upon dramatists who made open and direct attacks, since his "taxing like a wild-goose" might fly, "unclaimed of any man"; and, secondly, the passages in which the allusions occurred did not become dead wood which needed cutting out when the play was next revived and the events hinted at were forgotten; some of the meaning had evaporated, nothing worse. Of all the plays *Love's Labour's Lost* is that which abounds most in topicalities of this kind as it does also in indelicate innuendo, and those who obstinately hold to the doctrine of the impersonality and the respectability of Shakespeare should be condemned to edit that text until they had satisfactorily explained every allusion and every difficult reading.

But it is time I had done with criticising the portraits of Shakespeare by others and began my own.

It will, as is fitting, be a portrait in the renaissance style, though of an earlier period than that which stands at the beginning of this book. It will belong in manner to the Italian school which set its figures against a background of landscape and human occupation, of cloud-capped towers and solemn temples. And I shall begin by sketching this background first, not neglecting the central figure entirely, but showing it in outline only and leaving the details of posture, costume, face and expression to be filled in later. For though Shakespeare may be for all time, he was also very much of an age, and unless we grasp at least the main features of that age we are likely to miss much that is significant about him. Above all, his spiritual development, which is evident in the poems and plays, now we know their approximate order, can only be fully apprehended if we consider it in relation to the spiritual condition of the time in which he lived.

II

THE ELIZABETHAN SCENE

Infinite riches in a little room
Marlowe, *Jew of Malta.*

"THE SPACIOUS TIMES of great Elizabeth" has become a cliché since Tennyson first coined the phrase. Yet how "cabined, cribbed, confined", how "bound in to saucy doubts and fears" should we find ourselves in that world!

Shakespeare inhabited the diminutive, compact and tidy universe designed by Ptolemy fifteen hundred years before his day, and his very language is full of astronomical notions now long forgotten. This universe was a miracle of ordered harmony. A "pendent world", which included the whole starry space visible to man together with the containing Firmament, it hung like a jewel from the floor of Heaven, Hell lying beneath it and Chaos about it. Circular in shape, it comprised a system of transparent spheres, one within the other, in which were fixed the sun and moon, together with "those patens of bright gold" the stars, while the whole revolved at various speeds around "this centre" the earth, and in thus turning made music so ravishingly divine that mortals, closed in their "muddy vesture of decay", were unable to perceive it. We smile at this pretty little musical box, but it was more comforting to Man's pride and aspiration than our vast cosmos in which the earth is an infinitesimal atom. Of that old-time creation he was the masterpiece, "the beauty of the world, the paragon of animals"; and the grandeur and sublimity of Shakespeare's tragedies owe much to a sense of the kingly part Man was called upon to play "before high Heaven" on Earth, that central stage of a "wide and universal theatre".

Yet modern science, while reducing man to zero, has banished fear from his universe. In Shakespeare's limited cosmos fear met him at every turn. It only held together by keeping balance, harmony and an ordered hierarchy of degrees, corresponding with the angelic ranks about the Deity or the galaxy of nobles at an earthly court. Disturb this balance and at any moment the heavenly bodies might "start madly from their spheres"; and the dire effect of such "disasters" upon human affairs is described by Ulysses in the first act of *Troilus and Cressida*:

> Take but degree away, untune that string,
> And hark what discord follows! each thing meets
> In mere oppugnancy: the bounded waters
> Should lift their bosoms higher than the shores
> And make a sop of all this solid globe:
> Strength should be lord of imbecility
> And the rude son should strike the father dead.

The apprehension that the whole order might suddenly revert to Chaos haunted men's imagination; and is constantly in Shakespeare's thoughts.

> But I do love thee! and when I love thee not,
> Chaos is come again—

how much that cry of Othello's gains if we grasp what the Elizabethans meant by "the harmony of

16

the spheres"! The stars, again, "rained influence", and astrologers spent busy lives searching the skies for evidence of their sway over the fortunes of individuals and of states, while unaccountable phenomena, like eclipses, comets and meteors, were especially dreaded,

> As harbingers preceding still the fates,
> And prologues to the omen coming on.

The world moreover was the abode of myriads of evil spirits, classified by learned demonologists and assigned to their respective elements of earth, air, fire and water. Madness was due to "possession", and there was a recognised procedure for the exorcising of devils by properly qualified persons. Dealers in black magic on the other hand, with their familiars and attendant demons, were held in detestation by all honest persons, and if convicted were burnt without mercy. Practically every one in Shakespeare's time believed in witchcraft, and we have no reason for thinking that the creator of *Macbeth* was immune from the universal delusions of his age. Among these must be reckoned ghost-lore, which was a topic of burning controversy in the sixteenth century, some believing that ghosts were devils and others adhering to the medieval idea that they were the spirits of the departed. Technically, all spirits, except angels and those in bliss, were evil. But popular superstition made an exception in the case of fairies, holding that they were "spirits of another sort". It is significant of this difference that while the fairies belong to Shakespeare's comedies, especially to those serenest of all his plays,

A Midsummer-Night's Dream and *The Tempest*, his tragic world is inhabited by ghosts and witches.

It is significant too that the ghosts and the witches do not become prominent until his Jacobean days, or at any rate until after 1600. The subjects of Elizabeth had a gaiety of mind that the next reign lacked. The Englishmen of her age felt that they did indeed belong to "spacious times". They had a sense of release, of new horizons suddenly opened up, which must have been extraordinarily exhilarating. The Renaissance was essentially an assertion of the spiritual emancipation of man from the religion, the social structure, the scholasticism of the middle ages. And in England during the second half of the sixteenth century special circumstances gave the movement a peculiar quality. The establishment of a strong central government, brought peace and order into a land which had groaned under the anarchy of the Wars of the Roses—and the fear of a return to such anarchy lies at the back of all Shakespeare's historical plays. The breach with Rome, although half the people still hankered after the forms and doctrines of the "old religion", typified the immense quickening of national self-consciousness that culminated in the triumphant defiance of the Spanish supremacy. A new nobility arose to take the place of the feudal baronage that finally perished on Bosworth field, a nobility based upon wealth, often derived from church property, or on royal favour, readily bestowed upon a handsome face and taking manners. The weakening of the bonds of custom which had tied the lower orders to status and the soil since time immemorial, caused the highways suddenly to grow populous with vagabond rogues and "lawless resolutes". The rapid development of internal trade and overseas commerce gave increased power and wealth into the hands of an expanding middle class. The drawing aside of the curtain of mystery veiling the stage of the Atlantic revealed to man's astounded and delighted gaze a whole New World for discovery, plantation, and plunder. And all these varied threads were woven together on Time's loom to fashion a texture of thought and society, which seemed at once durable and pliant, shot with swiftly changing hues and yet serviceable for daily wear, offering on the one hand security and on the other adventure. It was this combination—almost unparalleled in history since the days of Pericles—of social stability with illimitable opportunity for the individual, which gave the Elizabethan age its sense of balanced flight, its unique quality of happiness and spontaneity. The whole world was in flux, and yet by some trick of magic men trod on solid ground.

Nor were the Elizabethans in any doubt who the magician might be. They turned, and rightly turned, in gratitude to their Queen. Their grandfathers had endured the social anarchy which marked the end of the middle ages. Their fathers had drunk to the dregs the cup of Geneva under Edward VI and the cup of Rome under Mary, and found neither to their taste. Yet no third alternative had appeared possible. Elizabeth, the procrastinator, the crowned sphinx who could never make up her mind, who reigned forty-five years perpetually hesitating between Protestantism and Catholicism, between peace and war, between marriage and virginity, provided the alternative—a breathing-space of nearly half a century for the English people to discover a middle way and to grow contented, prosperous and respected throughout the world. England at that time was the one peaceful country in a Europe ravaged by religious wars, in which she was willing enough to take part on French or Flemish soil; and the epoch lies like a miraculous season of calm weather between the Wars of the Roses and the Puritan Revolution. The Virgin Queen was worshipped by her subjects because she gave them stability, and when foreign ambassadors enquired the secret of it she danced before them. The stability of Elizabethan England was a balance.

Her court too was both the keystone and the symbol of the national life. The headquarters of a strong executive under the permanent direction of the Cecils, it was also a stage on which almost any young man who took the Queen's fancy might cut a figure and if he were lucky make a fortune. Fortunes were to be had because the Crown not only controlled the distribution of lucrative monopolies and such properties as came to it through intestacy, but also itself took part in those expeditions, half-commercial and half-piratical, to the New World and elsewhere which were so frequent at this time. Elizabeth lived on the Thames; her five chief palaces, Whitehall, Hampton Court,

Greenwich, Richmond and Windsor, all gave on to the river; and she passed from one to another in her royal barge. The goings and comings, therefore, of the great sea-captains Frobisher, Hawkins, and Drake, took place under her very windows; and when the last-named returned to Deptford in 1580 after his famous voyage round the world, she boarded the *Golden Hind* and knighted him on his own deck, beneath which, as she pretended not to know, lay ballast in the form of ingots plundered from the Pacific coast of Spanish South America.

Nor was the traffic confined to America. Any day a vessel might appear in the Thames laden with merchandise from Africa, from Muscovy, from the Levant, even from India or the Far East. For London, which had been an obscure port at the north-west corner of the medieval map, suddenly found herself the centre of the world. And during the last fifteen years or so of Elizabeth's reign, eyes and ears greater than hers drank in the sights and sounds of the little-great river. Shakespeare's plays are drenched in sea-spray and shot with the coloured thread of mariner's tales, from the pitiful story of old Aegeon in *The Comedy of Errors* to *Pericles*, *The Winter's Tale* and *The Tempest*, while the Venice of his *Merchant* is only London in masquing attire.

The British Empire was founded by private ad-venturers exploiting the outlying parts of the world, with the unofficial encouragement of Elizabeth. Modern English literature had a similar origin. The Renaissance, though a learned movement, had its true centre not in universities but at courts grown rich with commerce. In the fourteenth and fifteenth centuries it became the fashion for the merchant princes of Italy to devote their surplus wealth, the banking system being then still in its infancy, to the encouragement of art and literature, much of which possessed the double attraction of offering at once a permanent investment and a means of personal display. This fashion spread to the rest of Europe, and Chaucer was already benefiting from it before 1400. Elizabeth, therefore, inherited a long tradition of royal patronage of art and letters, and as a daughter of Henry VIII and Anne Boleyn she was fond both of learning and of pageantry. But she inherited also an exhausted treasury and a full share of her grandfather Henry VII's passion for economy. Thus she contrived to obtain as much entertainment as possible without spending a penny more upon it than she could help.

The arrangement as regards plays was that towards Christmas, at which season and up to Twelfth Night the court held high festival, the Master of the Revels, whose office was a special department of the royal household under the immediate charge of the Lord Chamberlain, invited the acting-companies of London to submit plays for selection, very much as Philostrate does in *A Midsummer-Night's Dream*. The players, of course, received a fee for performing the chosen play or plays; but the Queen had no direct financial responsibility for their maintenance, any more than she had for the expeditions of Drake and Hawkins.

Indeed the public theatres of the metropolis came into existence during the second half of her reign in order, at any rate in theory, to give scope for the companies to rehearse before performing at court, without being at the charge of Her Majesty. And the theory that the players existed for the Queen's "solace", as the phrase went, was of vital importance in other respects. The growing puritanism of the City rendered the Lord Mayor and Corporation bitterly hostile as a rule to the theatre, so that but for the protection of the Court the stage would have been suppressed long before Shakespeare reached London.

The poets, like the dramatists, looked to Elizabeth as towards the sun in their heaven; but she had in general small comfort to offer those who courted her in verse and were unable to support themselves by public means. Moreover, she herself took much greater delight in music than in poetry, and had as we have seen a passion for dancing. In this, as in so many other ways, she was typically English of the time. During the latter part of her reign music and dancing were even more popular than the drama itself, and a puritan writer in 1587 complains that "London is so full of unprofitable pipers and fiddlers that a man can no sooner enter a tavern than two or three cast of them hang at his heels, to give him a dance before he depart". In those days you were entertained to music while your barber shaved you, and it was counted a shame for a lady or gentleman to be unable to "bear a part" when, as the custom was, the music-books were brought in after supper and the company sat round the table to sing madrigals. This indeed was the golden age of English music, and especially of English vocal music, the age of the great polyphonic composers William Byrd, Thomas Campian, Orlando Gibbons, and a host of others. That Shakespeare was himself passionately fond of music is witnessed by the countless references to music and singing in his plays.

Most of the well-known composers were in the service of noblemen, and every Elizabethan gentleman of standing maintained musicians as part of his household, "the music of the house" as Nerissa calls it being as necessary to greatness in that day as gardeners and chauffeurs are in this. The Tudor peace transformed the private armies of the barons, the bane of medieval England, into retinues of servants which included musicians, players and entertainers of other kinds; and instead of fighting each other the nobility, like Duke Theseus, occupied such time as was not given to the chase and other sports,

With pomp, with triumph and with revelling.

The great country houses, indeed, were in many ways like petty courts, and writers as well as musicians and players looked to their owners for patronage. Nor can there be any doubt that English literature, which might have fared badly had it been solely dependent upon Gloriana and her minister Burleigh, who preferred history and divinity to poetry and drama, stands very much indebted to the noble patrons of that period. Elizabethan authors, especially second-rate authors, frequently complain of lack of patronage; and with the multiplication of poets, novelists and pamphleteers, a number of them, no doubt, looked up and were not fed. But all the best poets and dramatists of the age seem to have found patrons, though the form of assistance they received may not have been always to their liking.

The career of Spenser is instructive. At first attached to the retinue of the Earl of Leicester, probably at the instance of his friend Sir Philip Sidney, who was Leicester's nephew, he next became private secretary to Lord Grey of Wilton, the Lord Deputy of Ireland, after which he held in succession various posts under the Irish government and so came to spend the rest of his life on "salvage soil", save for brief visits to London, one of them undertaken at the advice of yet another patron, Sir Walter Raleigh, who insisted on *The Faerie Queene* being presented at Court, where it earned the poet less than his hopes, but at any rate a pension of fifty pounds a year, a by no means inconsiderable sum for those days. Ben Jonson, to take another example, enjoyed the friendship, hospitality, and financial help of many patrons, and the Earl of Pembroke was in the habit of sending him £20 (equal to about £200 in modern money) every New Year for the purchase of books for his study.

In general, there seem to have been three degrees of patronage. First, there was the fee or reward for the dedication of a book, which varied in amount from shillings to guineas according to the generosity of the patron or the value he put upon the author's effort. Noblemen and gentry were pestered by impecunious authors for such fees, and refusals were no doubt common; but the custom was a time-honoured one and important publications seldom went without their rewards, sometimes from several patrons. The number of dedicatory sonnets to great personages which preface *The Faerie Queene* suggest, indeed, that Raleigh made it his business to collect as many guineas at Court for his friend as he could. And if the book pleased and its author were found acceptable, the next degree might be attained, namely personal employment in the patron's service. The hospitality which Spenser found at Leicester House, Ben Jonson for five years with Lord D'Aubigny, Nashe in the Isle of Wight with the family of Sir George Carey, and John Florio as servant of the young Earl of Southampton, was not of course entirely gratuitous. Literary men might prove useful in a variety of ways: they could act as secretaries, as land agents, as tutors to the patron or his children; and, when the occasion arose, they might be called upon to provide the "book" for a masque, a play, or some other form of entertainment, such occasions ranging from a wedding in the family to the elaborate preparations necessary for a visit from Her Majesty on one of her annual progresses. But the ultimate goal of most authors' ambition was the third and last degree of patronage, the gift of a permanent office under government. Very few attained it. Spenser, we have seen, did so, but only at the price of exile in a land he hated; Marlowe seems to have secured some shady employment in connexion with Walsingham's secret police system, and it cost him his life; Lyly hoped for the reversion of the mastership of the Revels Office, and died hoping.

Patronage, then, was not merely a custom of the age, it was for most writers an economic necessity. Every author sought for a patron, and the best patrons on their side thoroughly appreciated the compliment. For they stood to gain more than the services referred to above, which were after all merely incidental. What Shakespeare offered Southampton, and what all writers offered their patrons, was eternity.

> Not marble, nor the gilded monuments
> Of princes, shall outlive this powerful rhyme;
> But you shall shine more bright in these contents
> Than unswept stone besmeared with sluttish time—

such was the bid, and the terms in which Shakespeare expresses it remind us that patronage and the elaborate memorial monuments of the age belonged to the same fashion and were prompted by the same desire: to be remembered by succeeding generations. The investment was of course a speculation, since the length of the eternity depended upon the quality of the writer. Southampton is said to have ventured £1000, and if so posterity has paid him interest on the capital at an increasing rate of immortality; for fortune gave him the pick of the market.

Fashion and egotism, however, were not the whole story. The more distinguished Elizabethan and Jacobean courtiers were men of taste and culture who admired literature for its own sake and were as good judges of true poetic quality as their successors are of the points of a race-horse. And well they might be, for many of them were poets themselves in a minor fashion, and to be capable of journeyman's work is to be in the right way to appreciate the craft of a master. It generally flattered their vanity no doubt to feel that they had in their service poets as good or better than those of any of their rivals, and they made every effort to secure them. Yet there can have been little vanity in Sidney's love for Spenser, and when Raleigh brought Spenser to London in 1589 with three books of *The Faerie Queene* in his cloak-bag, he was inspired, partly by the hope of prestige for himself and favour from his royal mistress in return for this treasure-trove from Ireland, but partly also by real enthusiasm for what he recognised as genius of the highest order. Indeed Raleigh had an excellent eye for a poet, and appears to have lent his patronage to Marlowe, Chapman and Matthew Roydon simultaneously, to say nothing of mathematicians like Harriot for the study of navigation. And if Raleigh had poets and dramatists at command, the head of the rival faction at Court, the Earl of Essex, did no less. Thus the Montagues and Capulets of London had their attendant literary coteries, a fact which exerted an influence upon the career of Shakespeare so far all too little regarded.

While a dramatist, like Jonson, might enjoy the personal patronage of one nobleman, the actors he wrote for would in all probability be playing in the name of another. Every acting company served a lord, and was obliged to perform under his name and style, the lord being legally responsible for it. This was in the nature of a police measure, and differed in kind from personal patronage. Yet the two often shaded off into each other. The company's lord, for example, would naturally call upon them for help in providing entertainment at his own house; on the other hand, another lord might engage them for a similar purpose; occasionally, too, we hear of performances given in the public playhouse at the request of some gentleman or other.

Acting at the houses of private persons was generally in the evening, because public performances took place in the afternoon. It must not, however, be supposed that noblemen did not attend the public playhouses, though it was unseemly for ladies to show themselves there. A special "room", or as we should say "box", was reserved for lords, and we are told that during part of 1599, Shakespeare's patron, the Earl of Southampton, with his friend the Earl of Rutland, "passed away the time merrily in going to plays every day". Furthermore, the seats in the galleries, which were of varying prices, were largely occupied by gentlemen and professional men of different sorts, a large number of them being students of the Inns of Court, who, as one of them, the poet Donne, tells us, were

Of study and play made strange hermaphrodites.

Much has been heard of the "groundlings", for the

most part prentices, who paid a penny to stand on the floor of the house. It has been too little recognised that the public theatres were in the main dependent upon the cultured classes of London.

What would strike a modern eye most about Shakespeare's theatre was its smallness. The auditorium of the Globe was probably about 55 feet square, that is approximately the size of a lawn tennis court; and this included the stage, which jutted right out among the audience, and was some 43 feet wide by about 27 feet long. The play was therefore performed almost in the middle of the theatre, the groundlings standing on three sides of the stage, which was raised three or four feet off the floor, while the seats for those who could afford them were ranged in three tiers of galleries round the walls, and in some theatres stools could even be hired for accommodation on the stage itself. The whole atmosphere must have been extraordinarily intimate and domestic, especially when we remember that the personnel both of the company and of the audience was far more permanent than anything conceivable in modern London. Each member of the cast would be as familiar to the spectators as the individuals of a local football team are to-day to a crowd on the home ground. Under such conditions acting and drama were very different from anything we know now. And to understand Shakespeare, to follow the swiftness of his thought, the delicacy of his poetic workmanship, the cunning of his dramatic effects, the intricacy of his quibbles, to appraise in short the infinite riches of his art, we must think ourselves back into that little room at the Globe or its predecessors, in which his dramas were first given by a team of players, moving and speaking on a bare platform surrounded by a ring of faces only a few yards away, faces in front, to right, to left, above, faces tense with interest at the new miracle that awaited them, the faces of the brightest spirits and keenest intelligences of his time.

Did space permit, I might say much of the instrument for which he composed his mighty dramatic symphonies, that threefold instrument, the Elizabethan stage, the full significance of which Shakespearian criticism is only now beginning to appreciate. I will instance but one of its features, by way of showing how it moulded the art that belonged to it. The absence of stage scenery meant that Shakespeare had to create it in the verse he wrote.

> But look, the morn, in russet mantle clad,
> Walks o'er the dew of yon high eastward hill,

said an actor playing Horatio, pointing across the Globe theatre one sunny afternoon in 1601; and the spectators were entirely unconscious of any incongruity. Can we do better with all the resources of a mechanical age? Rather, does not the shining splendour of those lines make even the best contrivance of illuminated back-cloth look garish and absurd? Lacking scenery, again, Shakespeare lacked visual aids to the localisation of his scenes.

31

Where does *Macbeth* open, on earth or in hell? or
the third act of *Julius Caesar*, before the senate house
or within it? or the first and second scenes of the
second act of *Romeo and Juliet*, inside the orchard of
Capulet or beyond the wall? The answer to all these
alternatives is that the action of Shakespeare's plays
proceeds within the bare framework of the Elizabethan theatre, which just because it is delocalised
allowed the dramatist a freedom denied to his
modern successors. And if such bareness be thought
a primitive crudity, let the military plays be con-
sidered, plays whose short fighting scenes followed
each other on the Elizabethan platform with all the
bustle and excitement of a battle-field seen simultaneously at many points, but are so sadly hampered
by a drop-curtain as to be almost unplayable under
our theatrical conventions. The supreme example of
the kind is, of course, *Antony and Cleopatra*, in which
the whole globe itself could be the scene because it
was written for the Globe. In that theatre a dramatist was bounded in a nutshell and could count
himself king of infinite space.

As with the theatre, so with the age. The "spa-
ciousness" of Elizabeth's reign was in the minds of
her subjects, not in their circumstances, most of
which would seem small or mean to our thinking.
No doubt the tiny city of London, with its spires
nestling about old St Paul's, with its green fields to
the north, and with the clear unembanked Thames
lined with the palaces of the Queen and her great
nobles, would seem very beautiful to us, could we
survey it, through the smokeless air, from the

trumpeter's hut surmounting the Globe on the southern Bankside, as Shakespeare himself had often done, and perhaps did in memory when writing Prospero's vision of towers and palaces and temples. But we should find much to offend nose and eye, to say nothing of humane feeling, in its narrow streets. With an aesthetic sensibility and discrimination that puts ours to shame, the Elizabethans combined a coarseness, brutality and physical insensitiveness, which it is essential to remember if we are to understand Shakespeare, whose growing abhorrence of these elements is the main key to his later development. And from the very beginning he brought from Stratford a delicate nose, which found the effluvia of London, human or otherwise, highly distasteful. Bodily ablutions and sanitation are inventions of nineteenth century England: a contemporary doctor advises his readers to confine their washing to the hands and wrists, to the face, the eyes, and the teeth, adding "in the night, let the windows of your house, specially of your chamber, be closed". Fresh air and sunlight were thought positively dangerous, ladies wearing masks to preserve their faces from the latter. Hygiene was in its infancy; the nostrums of medieval physic in their dotage. Surgery was a branch of the barber's art, and physiology was based upon the notion of humours which goes back to Hippocrates. In a word, man living in a pre-scientific age had no clue either to the prevention or to the cure of disease, with the result that the streets stank like middens, which indeed they were, and bubonic plague was an

33

annual visitant to the city. The danger of infection was, however, well recognised, and when the deaths from plague reached more than fifty a week the theatres were closed by authority. A particularly violent outbreak in 1593-4, which killed some ten to fifteen thousand persons, had, as we shall see, an important influence upon Shakespeare's career, and other visitations affected the fortunes of his company.

The streets were turbulent as well as filthy and unhealthy. At any moment the cry of "Clubs!" would collect a mob of prentice boys for battle, and the Southwark scene in 2 *Henry VI* which begins

> *Alarm and Retreat. Enter again Jack Cade and all*
> *his rabblement.*
>
> *Cade.* Up Fish-street, down St Magnus' Corner, kill and knock down, throw them into Thames—

was assuredly from the life. Nor were poor prentices the only cause of strife. The brawls between the retainers of Montagues and Capulets had their parallel in London, for serving-men knew which way the wind blew and were ready enough to express in the streets the mutual hatred of their masters. Fighting and sport were near kindred. Close to the Globe stood the Bear Garden at which bears might be seen baited by dogs on most afternoons of the week except Sundays, while a scarcely more edifying display was provided by cock-fights; both royal sports which Elizabeth graced with her presence when they were given at court.

Even the crude justice of the age lent its aid to mob-excitement and brutalisation. The grisly decapitated heads of traitors looked down on you as you passed over London Bridge; this jeering procession that meets you is a throng following a cart, tied to the back of which walks a bawd, with beadles whipping her bare and bloody back; and if you are lucky you may find your way to Tyburn where a public execution is toward, of all spectacles the best-beloved by a London crowd. For here at no cost except a few hours of waiting to secure a good station, you may see the hangman at his work, of which hanging is the least interesting part. It is a common traitor, we will suppose, some Jesuit caught in his vestments at mass by Master Richard Topcliffe, the head of the government secret police, an expert human ferret, and cunning at devising new tortures. The Popish recusant has been dragged to Tyburn upon a hurdle, and the hangman, you hear, is in good form, having already shown marvels of skill with his knife upon other traitors before your arrival. For the Elizabethan hangman is an artist, and the knife is his chief instrument; the art consisting in tossing his man off the ladder, hanging him, but cutting him down before he breaks his neck, so that he may be dismembered and disembowelled while still alive. Indeed there is one recorded instance of a priest who was heard praying while the hangman already had his bleeding palpitating heart in his hand—and skill could hardly go beyond that. Did Shakespeare ever attend executions of this kind? Not often, I think; yet Macbeth's cry, "As they had seen me with these hangman's hands!" shows that he could be present at least in imagination.

Less fascinating perhaps but more imposing was the pomp of executions for high treason, far the most important of which during Shakespeare's life in London being the beheading of Robert, Earl of Essex, on February 25, 1601, to which however the public were denied access, as it took place in the Tower. This portentous event, and not the death of the Queen in 1603, was the end of the true Elizabethan age, those halcyon days of happy ease, illimitable hope and untarnished honour, when Shakespeare was writing his great comedies and seemed able to turn a blind eye upon the squalor, the meanness, the bestiality around him. The brilliant but erratic young earl, the principal star in the Elizabethan firmament for the last ten years of the century, suddenly fell like Lucifer from heaven; and his catastrophe shook men's souls with terror and amazement as at some monstrous disaster in the skies. The sacred string of "degree" had been loosed; the harmony was broken; the Elizabethan balance overthrown. England awoke with a start to the grim realities of life, and the accession of James I ushered in a period of cynicism and gloom, self-indulgence and crime.

All this, we shall see, produced a profound effect upon Shakespeare. And how familiar it is to us! The modern world speaks a different language and has run a very different political course, but the mood of 1932 is almost exactly the mood of 1602;

for, though our material conditions are better, the height of our spiritual fall has been greater.

> Incertainty that once gave scope to dream
> Of laughing enterprise and glory untold,
> Is now a blackness that no stars redeem,
> A wall of darkness in a night of cold.

III

ENTER WILLIAM SHAKESPEARE
WITH DIVERS OF WORSHIP

What I have done is yours, what I have to do is yours, being
part in all I have, devoted yours
Shakespeare to the Earl of Southampton, 1594.

SHAKESPEARE DIED at the early age of fifty-two,
and history is almost completely silent concerning
the first twenty-eight years of his life. Here is the
meagre framework of certainties, drawn from
ecclesiastical records:

1564, Ap. 26. William, son of John Shakespeare, baptised at Stratford.

1582, Nov. 27 and 28. Entries in the Bishop of Wor-
cester's Register relating to the marriage of William
Shakespeare to Anne Hathway of Stratford, a woman
eight years his senior.

1583, May 26. Susanna, daughter to William Shakespeare, baptised at Stratford.

1585, Feb. 2. Hamnet and Judith, twin children to
William Shakespeare, baptised at Stratford.

Thus we do not know how or where he was edu-
cated, when he joined the stage, at what period he
went to London, or indeed anything at all of his
boyhood or of those early critical years of adult life,
beyond the fact of his marriage at eighteen to a
woman of twenty-six. And then suddenly in the
years 1592 to 1594 the curtain is drawn aside to discover him already at the height of fame and prosperity; as a leading actor in the leading company in
England, as a member of the most brilliant of court